Considering th  gaming as a p... and female alike, the subject has received very little attention among Christian thinkers and writers. For that reason and others I am thankful for this brief book and its level-headed, Bible-based teaching and counsel.

**Tim Challies**
Blogger at www.challies.com

From my teenage years, through college, and into marriage, video games were a steady part of my life. Issues arose when I failed to use wisdom when it came to gaming, and eventually I was trapped in sin as I neglected numerous priorities in favor of my virtual life. Video games aren't sinful, but without godly wisdom gaming can lead to sin. My friend Reagan Rose has given our generation a simple, practical, and biblical game plan that will allow you to enjoy gaming without neglecting the glory of God.

**Costi W. Hinn**
President & Founder of For the Gospel
www.forthegospel.org

It's hard not to arrive at the conclusion that twenty-first century society is addicted to distraction. Media companies have perfected the art and science of keeping us laser-locked on their products, often to the detriment of our other important duties. One realm of media that has taken over an entire generation is video gaming. Thankfully, there is help to be found. Reagan Rose has offered us a very timely, thoughtful, clear, and convicting book for young Christians who are engaged in the gaming world. With grace and wisdom, he navigates the topic carefully, but truthfully, the scope of this book goes even further. Not only did I finish reading the book with thankfulness, but I was motivated to examine all areas of my life in order to surrender them to the glory of God. Praise the Lord! This book belongs in the hands of every Christian.

**Nate Pickowicz**
Pastor, Harvest Bible Church, Gilmanton Iron Works, New Hampshire
Author of *How to Eat Your Bible*

In every generation, Christian parents face new parental issues that require careful biblical insight and vigilant navigation. Reagan Rose introduces one of those issues to parents and students alike and asks us to pull up a seat, lay down the controller, and open our Bible. *A Student's Guide to Gaming* not only assists parents in navigating the diverse issues surrounding video games, but it's for every student longing for superior satisfaction but who often settle for far less. With pastoral sensitivity and personal experience, Rose provides an excellent summation of the dangers and joys of gaming and how parents and students can learn to redeem the time for God's glory.

**Dustin Benge**
Provost and professor, Union School of Theology,
Bridgend, Wales

Believers are called to see every area of life through the lens of God's Word. This includes our entertainment. In *Gaming*, Reagan Rose takes us on a tour of the virtual world of video games, teaching us about its excitements, dangers, and opportunities. I read this book with my son and recommend it to anyone who plays video games or disciples those who do.

**Garrett Kell**
Pastor, Del Ray Baptist Church, Alexandria, Virginia
Author of *Pure in Heart: Sexual Sin and the Promise of God*

Gaming is a popular pass-time. So much of it is fun but pitfalls abound. In this short, simple resource, Reagan Rose offers biblical fuel for personal reflection and wider conversation on both the joys and the dangers. Packed with help and hope, there is encouragement here for gamers and their non-gaming family and friends. A real spur to honour Christ online.

**Helen Thorne**
Director of Training and Resources, Biblical Counselling UK

TRACK
CULTURE

**A STUDENT'S GUIDE TO GAMING**

# REAGAN ROSE

SERIES EDITED BY
JOHN PERRITT

CHRISTIAN
FOCUS

rtm

Copyright © Reagan Rose 2022

paperback ISBN 978-1-5271-0798-4
ebook ISBN 978-1-5271-0868-4

10 9 8 7 6 5 4 3 2 1

First published in 2022
by
Christian Focus Publications Ltd,
Geanies House, Fearn, Ross-shire,
IV20 1TW, Great Britain
www.christianfocus.com

with

Reformed Youth Ministries,
1445 Rio Road East
Suite 201D
Charlottesville,
Virginia, 22911

Cover by MOOSE77

Printed by Bell & Bain, Glasgow

# CONTENTS

Watch out for other forthcoming books in the
*Track* series, including:

# Series Introduction

Christianity is a religion of words, because our God is a God of words. He created through words, calls Himself the Living Word, and wrote a book (filled with words) to communicate to His children. In light of this, pastors and parents should take great efforts to train the next generation to be readers. *Track* is a series designed to do exactly that.

Written for students, the *Track* series addresses a host of topics in three primary areas: Doctrine, Culture, and the Christian Life. *Track's* booklets are theologically rich, yet accessible. They seek to engage and challenge the student without dumbing things down.

One definition of a track reads: *a way that has been formed by someone else's footsteps.* The goal of the *Track* series is to point us to that 'someone else'—Jesus Christ. The One who forged a track to guide His followers. While we cannot follow this track perfectly, by His grace and Spirit He calls us to strive to stay on the path. It is our prayer that this series of books would help guide Christ's Church until He returns.

In His service,

John Perritt
RYM's Director of Resources
Series Editor

# Introduction

Video games are everywhere, in our bedrooms, on our computers, and on the phones in our pockets. Ever since video games first appeared in the 1970s in dark corners of arcades, Christians have had an opinion about them.

Some believers only want to point out the negatives of video games: too violent, too time-consuming, too worldly. But others only highlight the positives: their artistic value or how they teach problem solving skills. But for many believers, we're somewhere in the middle. Video games are just another kind of entertainment. What's the big deal?

So, how should a Christian student think about video games and the place they have in our lives? Is it something we shouldn't waste time thinking about? Should we swear them off completely? I believe the answers can only be found if we make sure we are asking the right questions.

Usually, when Christians are discussing the merits of video games, they ask whether video games are good or bad. But I believe that's the wrong question to start with. If we really want to think deeply about where video games should fit into a Christian's life, we should start with a deeper question, *why are video games fun?* Because it is a fact, video games are a ton of fun!

Whether you are a gamer or not, the statistics are clear: people young and old love video games. Their draw is unlike any media we have ever seen before. In the United States, the video game industry is worth more than even the Hollywood movie industry. Yes, video games are a big medium for entertainment, but there is something unique about video games, that is not shared by movies, books, TV, or any other type of media: **Video games invite us to participate in the action.**

I'm convinced that the participatory nature of video games is part of what makes them so enjoyable, but it's also the reason we should scrutinize them carefully. Acting out stories, competing, or just living in a virtual world can be incredibly fun and have many benefits, but they also present potential obstacles which ought to be considered by anyone serious about following Christ.

Understanding why video games are fun is a matter of diving into the human heart. What does God say we were made for? What drives our deepest longings and how do video games promise to fulfill those desires?

This book examines video games from a biblical perspective and shows how the very things we find enjoyable about games actually point to our ultimate, God-given purpose while simultaneously threatening to thwart it. If you've ever struggled to stop gaming once you've started or if you wonder about the effects the content in your games is having on you, I think you'll be surprised at some of the answers.

This book is not anti-video games. But Christians must consider video games in light of the mission God has given us here on earth. I don't believe video games are bad. In fact, it's precisely the opposite. My concern is that video games may actually be too good.

# 1. Video Games Are Too Good

_'All things are lawful for me,' but not all things are helpful. 'All things are lawful for me,' but I will not be dominated by anything._
_(1 Cor. 6:12)_

Lilly was obsessed with the game _Fortnite_. She would watch her older brother play all the time. Eventually he let her play a few matches. At first it was really hard, but each time she played she got a little better. Once she finally won a match, though, all she wanted was to win again.

She would play whenever she had opportunity: after school, on the weekends, and even in the morning before breakfast. The boys at school thought it was cool that a girl was into _Fortnite_, and that extra attention made Lilly want to play all the more. But after a few weeks, _Fortnite_ became the only thing Lilly wanted to do.

Lilly's parents soon noticed that she was spending every free moment gaming. And if she wasn't playing *Fortnite*, she was talking about it or drawing pictures of it on her homework assignments. Lilly's grades began to slip. Teachers began sending notes home to her parents with words like 'disengaged,' 'irritable,' and 'distracted.' So, Lilly's parents limited her to only thirty minutes of *Fortnite* per day. This made Lilly mad, madder than her parents had ever seen her before.

Lilly begrudgingly complied with the new rule, at least for a little while. But after a few days she started sneaking out of her room in the middle of the night to play. 'One more match,' she would tell herself. But one would turn into ten. Soon the morning sun would be leaking through the window and Lilly would carefully tiptoe back to bed before her parents woke up.

Before *Fortnite* Lilly had been an excellent student, sibling, and daughter. She was even in the habit of reading her Bible every morning. But after she started sneaking in her all-night gaming sessions, her grades began to slip. She started snapping at her parents and brother over the smallest things, and she completely stopped reading her Bible.

What happened? How did Lilly's love for a game turn into such a problem? How did video games become so important to her that she would neglect everything else?

What happened to Lilly obviously doesn't happen to everyone who loves video games, but it is an oddly common occurrence. People will often point to stories like Lilly's as examples of how bad video games are. That's not what I want to do. In this chapter, we're not going to talk about what makes video games bad, but what makes them good—so good that if we aren't careful, they can take over our lives.

## GAMES HAVE CHANGED

Growing up I loved video games. I remember Saturday mornings walking across the dew-covered grass to my neighbor's house to play *Duck Hunt* and *Super Mario Bros.* on their Nintendo Entertainment System. These games were pretty simple. We would play for an hour or two, get bored and move on to watching cartoons or, if it was warm enough, playing baseball in the park. Video games were fun, but they weren't our life. The games just weren't good enough to hold your attention for hours on end.

When I reached college, however, I got into online gaming. And like Lilly, once I started,

I would find it nearly impossible to stop playing. My studies, relationships, and other responsibilities suffered. The games I played were just so gripping. They held my attention and kept me coming back for more. Today's video games are incredibly good, but sometimes that can actually be a bad thing.

Video games are a big part of many students' lives, they talk about them with friends, daydream about them in school, and when they're not playing, they're often watching other people play them over livestream or on YouTube. Games are everywhere, and they are more engaging than ever.

If you've ever lost your temper when someone walked in front of the screen, gotten annoyed when your Mom made you put your phone away at dinner, or didn't know what to do with yourself when the Wi-Fi was down, you know just how hard it is to stop playing once you've started. But have you ever wondered why that is? Why are video games so enthralling?

## DESIGNED TO ADDICT

Video game developers purposefully design their games to keep you playing. It's just good business. It used to be that the way a game developer made money was almost exclusively through selling copies of games. In the old days, arcades were the focus of the developer but later sales were done directly to consumers. Once you owned the game, you were no longer a potential customer for that game, and they had to market new games to you if they wanted more of your money. These were the types of video games I grew up with. The consoles and computers were not even connected to the internet, so there were no such things as in-app purchases, monthly subscriptions, or downloadable content. These are all new ways game developers have come up with to draw more money from their existing player base. As a result, these early games were fun, but they were not nearly as fun as modern games. Because developers had no financial incentive to keep you playing as long as possible. But that's all changed.

For major game publishers like Activision Blizzard over half of their revenue comes – not from game sales – but from in-game purchases.[1]

---

1   Bitner, Jon. 'Activision Blizzard Made Over $1 Billion From Microtransactions In Three Months.' *The Gamer.* https://www.thegamer.com/activision-blizzard-made-1-billion-microtransactions-three-months/. Accessed April 29, 2021.

And for most mobile games, that percentage is even higher. Or consider how many games have subscriptions or how many 'free' mobile games generate revenue through running ads.

Nearly all modern video games have tied their business strategy to how many hours they can keep people playing the game. *The more you play, the more they get paid.* But why should you care about this? Because it means it is in the best financial interest of game publishers to get you addicted to their games.[2] And game developers are not shy about this fact. Many of them openly admit that they are trying to find ways to make their games as addictive as possible.[3]

In just the past few years, the topic of video game addiction has gained wider attention in the psychological community. Researchers have begun to notice some gamers exhibiting

2   Balakrishnan, Janarthanan, and Mark D. Griffiths. 'Loyalty towards Online Games, Gaming Addiction, and Purchase Intention towards Online Mobile in-Game Features.' *Computers in Human Behavior* 87 (October 2018): 238–46. https://doi.org/10.1016/j.chb.2018.06.002.

3   In their book *Rules of Play: Game Design Fundamentals*, authors by Katie Salen Tekinbas and Eric Zimmerman actually admit that developers are deliberately trying to make games addicting, 355–56.

the exact same behaviors that have been observed in gambling addicts for years.

The World Health Organization now has an entry for 'gaming disorder' listed under addictive behaviors. It is described as:

> *impaired control over gaming, increasing priority given to gaming over other activities to the extent that gaming takes precedence over other interests and daily activities, and continuation or escalation of gaming despite the occurrence of negative consequences.*[4]

Sounds a bit like Lilly, doesn't it?

*The fact that people in secular medicine are concerned about the dangers of video game addiction should give us pause.* But as Christians, we want to know what God has to say about video games and addiction.

## ADDICTION AND THE GREATEST COMMANDMENT

Did you know the Bible never uses the word 'addiction?' That doesn't mean it doesn't address the subject, however. When the Bible talks about what we would call addiction it doesn't use the cold language of modern

---

4   'WHO | Gaming Disorder.' Accessed October 29, 2020.
    http://www.who.int/features/qa/gaming-disorder/en/.

psychologists. Instead, God uses much stronger language, words like 'slavery' and 'idolatry.' This issue of addiction is not really a medical issue at all. As Edward Welch says, 'the Bible traces addiction not to the body but to the soul.'[5]

We might be tempted to think that video game addiction isn't that big of a deal. After all it's not hurting anyone or destroying our bodies like drugs or other addictions. But when you understand addiction as a spiritual problem, then you start to see that it's not just about the physical destruction addictions can cause. It's much bigger than that. 'Addictions are ultimately a disorder of worship.'[6]

The primary reason we should want to be wary of becoming addicted to video games is not because of the harm it can cause to us (though it certainly can do that). The primary reason Christians should be cautious about *anything* that has the potential to become addictive is because it dishonors God. If addiction is a matter of worship, then the real horror of video game addiction is that it trades

---

5    Edward Welch, *Addictions: A Banquet in the Grave: Finding Hope in the Power of the Gospel* (P&R, 2001) 11.

6    Ibid., xvi.

the living God for the idolatry of a flickering screen.

## HOW EVEN GOOD THINGS CAN BECOME SINFUL

If all the evidence points to the fact that video games have the potential to be addictive, then we would be wise to approach gaming with the caution we use for other things that have the potential to ensnare us. It's not that video games are bad in and of themselves; the danger (and the sin) comes when we allow games to become the center of our lives instead of God.

We are commanded to 'love the Lord, your God, with all your heart and with all your soul and with all your might' (Deut. 6:5). Jesus said this is the first and greatest commandment (Matt. 22:37-38). But if our love has been captured by something less than Christ, even if that thing is not bad in and of itself, then we have sinned against God who is worthy of *all* of our worship.

If you think you might be struggling with addiction to video games, there is hope. The way to dislodge an idol of the heart is to replace it with something better. When our hearts and minds are filled with the beauty of Jesus Christ, there will be no place left for pixelated idols.

But that process will look different for each person.

Since video games are designed to be addicting, Christians must be cautious when we engage with them. Next, let's look at why it's so important that we don't allow games to take over our lives. What is it we are here for anyway?

## Main Point

*Video games are designed to keep us playing for as long as possible, so we need to be cautious.*

## Questions for Reflection

- What is your favorite game? What are some of the features that makes it so fun?
- Do you ever find it hard to stop playing certain games once you've started? What is it about them that makes you not want to stop?
- Why do you think video game addiction was less common among people in previous generations?

# 2. You've Been Given a Quest

---

*I have been crucified with Christ. It is no longer I who live, but Christ who lives in me. And the life I now live in the flesh I live by faith in the Son of God, who loved me and gave himself for me.*
*(Gal. 2:20)*

One of the most popular types of video game is the roleplaying game (RPG). Traditionally set in a medieval fantasy world, RPGs require the hero to develop skills and accomplish various quests. It might mean slaying a dragon, saving a princess, or exploring a dungeon, but there's always a quest or mission.

Most RPG quests start the same way: a non-player character gives you a mission which you agree to in exchange for a reward. You've just signed up for a quest. It will require preparation, it will require overcoming obstacles, and it will most certainly require you to avoid distractions to complete it, but in the end the reward will be well worth the trouble.

When you sign up to be a Christian you are saying yes to the greatest quest of all time. You are repenting of your sins, trusting in Christ's sacrifice, and acknowledging that Jesus is Lord over all, including your life. It's agreeing with God that your life is not your own and offering all of it to Him as a living sacrifice (1 Cor. 6:19-20; Rom. 12:1-2). The King of the universe has set you free from sin but He has also set you on a quest. This quest will require preparation, there will be obstacles to overcome, and there will be distractions that tempt you to abandon the mission. But in the end, the reward will be well worth it.[1]

Distractions are everywhere, aren't they? In an RPG, for example, there is the big quest that makes up the main story line, but there are also side quests you can undertake. These unrelated adventures are easier to accomplish but they pay out much smaller rewards than the main quest. And while these side quests might be fun and moderately rewarding, if you spend

---

1    For more on this quest, check out the *Justification*, *Sanctification* & *Glorification* booklets in the Track series.

all your time engaging in these diversions, you will never beat the main quest.

I think for some Christians, video games themselves can become like a side quest, a diversion from the main mission of life. That can happen with anything, not just video games. Entertainment is not necessarily sinful, but it needs to be put in its proper place. Anything—a job, a hobby, or video games—can get in the way of the mission Jesus has given us, if we let it. The quest of the Christian life is far too important a mission to be sidetracked by anything else. But what exactly is the quest of the Christian life? What are we supposed to be doing with our time here on earth?

## MISSION ACCEPTED

If you asked a room full of believers what the mission of the Christian life is, you would likely get a variety of responses. Some might say the mission is to help those in need, others might say it's to proclaim the gospel to the lost, still others would suggest the goal is simply to avoid sinning. Those things are all true to some degree, but they are only aspects of the main quest. The Westminster Shorter Catechism summarizes the Christian's mission simply: 'The chief end of man is to glorify God and enjoy Him forever.' Your mission is to glorify God. But have you accepted the mission?

One of the worst things in a game is that feeling when you reach the end of a level and realize you have forgotten to bring some crucial item. But in real life the stakes are much higher. If you reach the end of this life and have not obtained the most important possession of all, it really is game over for you—eternally. So, to even begin the quest of the Christian life, you have to first have Jesus Christ. He is not an optional add-on, and you need Jesus not just for the mission He gives you, but because you've got a serious problem.

## THE RED RING OF DEATH

Microsoft's Xbox 360, released in 2005, was supposed to be a revolutionary gaming console. But the early versions were plagued by a manufacturing flaw. The Red Ring of Death as it came to be known was the thing every Xbox 360 owner dreaded. The console had a circle of four indicator lights on the front which normally blink green in various patterns indicating the system was functioning properly. But the Red Ring of Death (or RROD for short) was when all four lights turned ominously red. When that happened, it was game over. Your shiny new video game console would never turn on again.

This problem was so widespread that Microsoft had to create an exchange program and explain to customers what had gone wrong. It turns out the RROD failure was due to an inferior material being used to bond some of the internal components in place. As the system would heat up during extended game play a specific bonding point would become soft and eventually it would completely break. This usually caused a horrible grinding noise as it put a deep, disk-ruining scratch into whatever game you happened to be playing at the time (R.I.P., my copy of *Halo 3*). And just like that your video console was transformed into a $500 doorstop. Every Xbox 360 owner had heard stories about the RROD and prayed it wouldn't happen to them. But if you played long enough, it was inevitable. There was a flaw in the system.

The Red Ring of Death was due to a flaw in the machine's design. Mankind has a flaw too, though it is not due to any negligence on the part of our Designer. Every human being is born pre-broken due to sin. We have all inherited the guilt of the first man, Adam, who sinned against God (Romans 5:12). And we have been complicit in this rebellion against our Maker ever since.

Daily we sin against God, choosing our desires over His commands. No one can argue that they have not. God's Word says we are all guilty: 'for all have sinned and fall short of the glory of God' (Rom. 3:23). And this sin has damning consequences. 'For the wages of sin is death' (Rom. 6:23).

A wage is what you are owed; what you deserve for your work. But the wages we have earned aren't a sack of digital gold pieces, or a +10 sword; it's death—eternal death. Apart from Christ we are all destined for eternal doom.

This seemingly severe consequence is because God, being a just judge, will not allow mankind's rebellion to go unpunished. He created us for a mission: to bring Him glory. But instead, we have marred the image of God by choosing sin. A day is coming when God will judge every person who has ever lived, and we will all get what we are owed (Heb. 9:27). And the terrifying news is that there is nothing we can do about it on our own. No number of good deeds, prayers, or church services will save us. It is entirely hopeless in our own strength. There is no way out.

That is, unless God makes a way.

## GOOD NEWS

The good news is that God has made a way for sinners like us to be saved from this destiny. Our problem is that we need to be forgiven, and we need to be righteous. To be righteous simply means that your life and attitudes are perfectly conformed to God's standards. The problem, as we have seen, is that we don't meet God's standards—we have fallen short. But how can a broken creature become righteous in God's sight, if we've already fallen short?

What is needed then is a substitute. If you are going to be made righteous in God's eyes, someone needs to stand in your place to take the punishment you deserve (remember, the wages of sin is death). Someone must fulfill the righteousness required to be acceptable in God's sight. The good news of the gospel should really be called the great news, because it announces that someone has indeed come to stand in the place of sinners like us!

Jesus Christ is that substitute. Two thousand years ago, God the Father sent His only Son, Jesus, into the world as a human. This was a rescue mission born out of love (John 3:16). Jesus lived a perfectly righteous life, never sinning, and always obeying. And He died as a sacrifice to pay the wage of death that sinners owed to God. Jesus came so that unrighteous sinners like you and me could be forgiven for our sins and obtain a right standing before God. And Jesus rose from the dead three days later, proving that He was who He said He was and defeating death. So now all who trust in Him can be forgiven, declared righteous, and have eternal life.

If you repent of your sin and believe in Jesus you become united to Him in such a way that when God looks on you, He sees Christ's death as atoning for your sins and His righteousness as counting toward your account. Then we are no longer like the Xbox 360, flawed and destined for destruction. In Christ, we have forgiveness, righteousness, and eternal life! 'For as in Adam all die, so also in Christ shall all be made alive' (1 Cor. 15:22). And you also receive that great life's mission. But if you don't start with Christ, the quest to glorify God with your life will be entirely fruitless.

## CONCLUSION

Putting your faith in Jesus Christ is just the beginning of the quest. Once we are in Christ by faith, we are then equipped to fulfill our purpose, to glorify God with our lives. The rest of the life of a Christian is living out that mission in God's power.

On this epic journey, the biggest danger is that we would forget that mission or be put off course by lesser things. The world is so full of distractions, and video games can become one of those distractions. They have the potential to enslave us and draw us away from what God has called us to do. That's really the whole point of this book. If our gaming has the potential to hinder our pursuit of glorifying God, then we need to scrutinize the place we will allow games to occupy in our lives. Games are great to enjoy in their proper place, but we have to be on the lookout for side quests that take the place of the main quest.

We've talked about addiction and the mission God has given us, but let's take it a layer deeper. What *exactly* is it about video games that makes us love them so much? Why are they so enthralling? What desires in our hearts are video games seeking to satisfy? If we can better understand what it is in games that captures our hearts, we will see how the true object of those longings is really found in Christ.

## Main Point

*God has given us the greatest mission of all, and we must be careful to not be distracted by lesser missions.*

## Questions for Reflection

- Are you a Christian? How do you know?
- Do you ever feel like other things can distract you from following Christ like you should?
- What are some things you can do to keep yourself focused on the main mission?

# 3. You Were Designed for Dominion

---

*And God said to them, 'Be fruitful and multiply and fill the earth and subdue it, and have dominion over the fish of the sea and over the birds of the heavens and over every living thing that moves on the earth.'*
*(Gen. 1:28)*

I used to play a phone game where you ran a quaint little bakery. The goal was to make cute cartoon pastries, raise profits, cut costs, and deal with precious little emergencies. After playing for a week everything was running smoothly in my virtual bakeshop. I felt really good that I was doing so well. Sure, I'd put in a lot of hours to reach this level, but all my hard work was finally paying off! I was succeeding.

One day I was playing the game at home when I paused it to get a drink. As I took a sip of my water and looked out the kitchen window to rest my eyes, I saw my neighbor building a shed in his backyard. It got me thinking about all of the projects around the house that I'd been putting off. In that moment I had this sinking realization: *What did I have to show for all the hard work I put into that video game?* Nothing.

As we discussed in the first chapter, video game developers want to make games as addictive as possible. But their efforts would not work unless we were already predisposed to want what they are offering. Video games are so engaging because they have the ability to latch on to something deep within us.

In the next few chapters, we will look at three longings the Lord has placed in our hearts. These desires are good, and God created them to be satisfied. But we will see how video games answer those yearnings by providing a fake substitute. The three heart-longings that video games seek to satisfy through simulation are **dominion**, **fellowship**, and **reward**. Or put another way, we were made for rule, relationships, and reward. Let's talk about rule first.

## DEFINING DOMINION

We all have the drive to build, make, overcome, solve, subdue, and conquer. There's something in us that craves bringing order to the world around us. Whether it's building houses, designing artwork, organizing, or writing computer code, people were created to create.

We often don't think about things this way, but I believe this is one of the main attractions of video games, especially for young men. Games present contained worlds that allow us to solve problems, overcome obstacles, and build to our heart's content. And something about that is immensely satisfying. It's what makes games fun to play. But have you ever wondered why you have that drive? What is it that makes us want to make things, to be competitive, and aspire to succeed? It's a hunger for dominion, and it's a desire God put in us.

Take a look at Genesis 1:27-28. This important passage describes what God created mankind to do. This is why we're here.

*So God created man in his own image, in the image of God he created him; male and female he created them. And God blessed them. And God said to them, 'Be fruitful and multiply and fill the earth and subdue it, and have dominion over the fish of the sea and over the birds of the heavens and over every living thing that moves on the earth.'*

After creating them, God gives a handful of related commands to Adam and Eve. Their mission is:

- Be fruitful
- Multiply
- Fill the earth
- Subdue it
- Have dominion over the creatures

In short, God created humans to rule as kings and queens over the earth. Theologians have given this command to rule a few different names but it's commonly termed 'the creation mandate' or 'the *dominion* mandate.' As the pinnacle of God's creation, God's original design was for us to glorify Him by ruling and reigning on the earth. That, I believe, is why deep within you there is this desire to build, to win, and to organize. It's what God made you to do.

A creature is always happiest when it is doing what it was made to do. And since dominion was what we were made for, exercising dominion brings us joy. When we build something, conquer a foe, or bring order where there was once chaos, we are doing what we were fashioned for. This is why victory tastes so sweet, and I'm convinced it's part of the reason why we love video games.

Think about a time when you beat a really hard level in a game, came in first place in a multiplayer match, or created something you were proud of in a building game. It felt great, didn't it? That was because you were scratching the itch of dominion. But dominion exercised in video games can never fully satisfy us.

## SIMULATED SUCCESS IS AN ILLUSION

But wait. If we are designed to dominate, and video games offer an opportunity to exercise that dominion, isn't that a good thing? If video games allow us to do what we were made to do and have fun while doing it, why would that be a problem? The problem is that video games are only a simulation. We cannot exercise meaningful dominion in video games because video games are not real.

Think about it, if we spend our strength and God-designed desire to dominate on something that isn't real, we aren't using it on things that really matter, things that bring God glory. When we invest all of our drive into something like video games which are not real and offer no lasting results for all our efforts, that is a failure of stewardship. But why is this imitation dominion still so enjoyable? The rip-off rule offered by games is attractive to us precisely because it isn't real.

When you try to build something in the real world, there are certain risks involved. You might make a fool of yourself, lose your money, or get hurt. That's the price of exercising dominion in a fallen world. But video games offer all the thrills of rule without any of the dangers. You can always turn the game off.

Video games offer what I call **simulated success**. Simulated success promises the thrill without the risk or the pain. But that also means that unlike dominion in the real world, simulated success has no real reward waiting for you when you win. Video games are certainly safe, but the success we enjoy in them is ultimately fruitless. This does not mean that they don't have any merit, but we must be cautious about this illusion of simulated success.

It makes sense why we would be drawn to an adventure game rather than a real-life adventure, doesn't it? Adventure is unsafe and uncertain, it's terrifying and it's risky. On a real adventure you could die. Much safer to slay a pretend dragon than fight a real one.

We are drawn to fantasy stories and games because we were made for dominion; we were made to do great things. But great things are dangerous. So, we redirect that innate desire toward make-believe to satisfy the longing for dominion while avoiding the risk.

In the real world, in order to succeed we have to face the thistles and thorns of the curse (Gen. 3:18). We have to take on risk and potential embarrassment should we fail. But if I lose in a video game, I might be disappointed, but I haven't really lost anything real. I can always start over.

But I'm convinced that indulging in the dummy dominion of video games will be bad for us in the long run. No real risk means no real reward. I also fear we might be doing damage to our God-given drive and work ethic by only tossing ourselves the softballs of imaginary challenges with simple answers; puzzles that were made to be solved and challenges with pre-built solutions created by developers. Real life is never so simple.

It's also this illusory quality of games that makes them ultimately unfulfilling and keeps us coming back again and again. We are always chasing the high of simulated success, but when we take hold of it, it always slips through our fingers like the vapor it is. Video games can be so fun, but if we're looking for fulfillment in them, they will always leave us feeling empty.

## SIMULATED SUCCESS OFFERS SIMULATED SATISFACTION

I sometimes wonder what I've lost by having given so much of my time to video games. How many opportunities to glorify God by imaging Him through my creativity have I forsaken? What might my life look like today if I had better invested the years of my youth in productive labor, instead of wasting thousands of hours on the simulated success of video games?

There are young men and women today who, in ages past, would have been the ones contriving expansive gardens, erecting great cities, or raising families. But instead our generation is hunched over our devices stacking pretend blocks in *Minecraft* and nurturing imaginary animals on our iPhones. What an awful exchange we've made: sham for substance.

Games are a sterilized version of real work and real accomplishment. Whatever success we enjoy in a game is always ultimately fleeting. It's just changing a number on a computer somewhere, data in a machine. And in the final analysis, whatever we achieve in our games will someday be forgotten, deleted, or replaced; burnt up like so much wood, hay, and stubble (1 Cor. 3:12-13). Those accomplishments may be entertaining now, but since that success is only a simulation, it will not last into eternity. And that's the real problem with dummy dominion, it's not only that we sacrifice the opportunity to enjoy the fruits of our labor in this life; the real horror is that we are relinquishing eternal reward.

## CONCLUSION

You were designed for dominion. The simulated success of video games will draw you in, but it will never satisfy your thirst. Play games in moderation, but don't let their siren song draw you to the rocks of addiction and a wasted life. Seek your satisfaction in something that can actually satisfy you. Fulfill that God-given desire for dominion. Build something, bring order to the world, take real risks in your studies and in your work and in your service to the Lord Jesus Christ. What you'll find is that real dominion is hard, but it will give you real satisfaction, and in eternity, real reward. More on that in chapter five. But for now, let's turn to the subject of relationships.

## Main Point

*Video games are fun because God designed us to overcome obstacles, create things, and exercise dominion.*

## Questions for Reflection

- Have you ever built something you've been really proud of? What was it and how did it make you feel?
- Where do you see simulated dominion in some of your favorite games?
- Have you ever felt like simulated success was robbing you of the desire to build or create things in the real world? When?

# 4. Be Careful of Fake Fellowship

———

*It is not good for man to be alone.*
*(Gen. 2:18)*

I met Cameron while leading a Bible study for students that met in the lounge of a college dormitory. Each week, before the study began, I'd come early and go room to room, knocking on doors, and asking students to join us. One week I ran into Cameron on the stairs just as I was finishing my rounds. I invited him to the Bible study, and with a smile he agreed to come.

Cameron was quiet during the study, but afterwards he came over to talk with me. He told me how glad he was that he came to the Bible study that day. I learned that he grew up in a Christian home, but he admitted to me that he had not even tried to find a church since moving away for college. He was relieved that the Lord had brought some Christians to him. The conversation ended with him saying he couldn't wait to be at the study next week.

But Cameron didn't come back to our study the next week, or the week after that. In fact, it would be weeks before I ever even saw Cameron again. And when I finally did run into him in the hallway, he apologized for missing the studies. I asked him if everything was okay. He said yes, but that he had other commitments that interfered. These other commitments, I learned, were to an online video game.

Cameron was nothing if not honest. He was very open about this with me. He told me how heavily invested he was in a certain massive multiplayer online role-playing game and how much his clan depended on him for their raid parties, some of which were scheduled for the same time our study met. I asked a few more probing questions and Cameron admitted that he hadn't really made any friends since coming to college because he'd been playing so much. That was one of the reasons he was so excited about our study, it was a chance to make some Christian friends.

I was amazed. Even though Cameron lived with a roommate, in a dorm full of other students, on a campus surrounded by people, and with a Bible study that met weekly in his own building, his only friends were on the computer. He had been so open with me so far, that I chanced a bold question. I asked, 'Cameron, do you think that is a good way to live?' And I'll never forget his answer. He said, 'I'm not sure, but having online friends is just so much *safer.*' And I knew exactly what he meant.

## FORMED FOR FELLOWSHIP

When God created mankind, He made us to have fellowship with other people. He said to Adam in Genesis 2:18, 'It is not good for man to be alone.' And that's why He gave him a wife. When Jesus established the Church, He designed a community. Nearly all of the letters in the New Testament were written to churches, and most of them address communities, not just individuals. And the majority of the commands that New Testament believers are called to obey involve us interacting with other people.

We've been called to love one another (1 John 4:7) and to not neglect meeting with other believers so that we can encourage one another (Heb. 10:25-26). It is impossible to live obediently before God if we isolate ourselves from others. And, like Cameron, we all feel that instinctive desire to be close to other people. But there is another feeling that often pulls us away from relationships and causes us to want to hide. If you've ever felt that tension between wanting to be close to people but not too close, you're not alone. There's a reason you feel that way.

While God created us for fellowship with other people, because of our sin we are filled with a sense of shame. Do you remember what the first thing Adam and Eve did after they ate from the fruit of the tree that the Lord forbade them? They hid. 'Then the eyes of both were opened, and they knew that they were naked. And they sewed fig leaves together and made themselves loincloths.' (Gen. 3:7). They felt shame, both before each other and before God. When God returned, they hid from Him too (3:8). Because of their sin, Adam and Eve felt shame for the first time and their relationship became strained. And since we all have sinned, we likewise all feel that same sense of shame before others.

Our sense of sin/shame is why relationships are so often fraught with misunderstandings, fights, disagreements, and hurt feelings. It is why the ones who you let get the closest are also the ones who can wound you the deepest. Anyone who has ever been betrayed by a friend or loved one knows the pain a broken relationship can bring. Is it any wonder, therefore, that we are often tempted to recoil and hide from close relationships altogether?

But what does any of this have to do with video games?

## A PLACE TO HIDE

Video games offer us a place to hide from the danger of being hurt by relationships. And online games take it a step further by allowing us to have a taste of the fellowship we so crave, but to have it on our terms. This social component is one reason online games tend to be more addictive.[1] People like Cameron turn to video games as a way to avoid the awkwardness and potential pain of real-life relationships. Online, you can hide behind an avatar, handle, or pseudonym. You can be you, but with a mask on.

---

1   Smohai, Máté, Róbert Urbán, Mark D. Griffiths, Orsolya Király, Zsuzsanna Mirnics, András Vargha, and Zsolt Demetrovics. 'Online and Offline Video Game Use in Adolescents: Measurement Invariance and Problem Severity.' *The American Journal of Drug and Alcohol Abuse* 43, no. 1 (January 2, 2017): 111–116.

Don't get me wrong, I'm not saying you shouldn't have friends online. But for someone like Cameron, whose only friends were online, he was only experiencing a shadow of the kind of relationships God designed him for. He was hiding from true fellowship by retreating to riskless relationships; friendships that allowed him to hide and only reveal as much of himself as he wanted. And if things ever got too real, he could always disconnect and disappear. But that is not the way God designed us to live.

I worry that online relationships will fulfill you just enough to keep you from pursuing the more tangled real-life relationships that God has called us to. You might find your desire for relationship met by online friends, and disengage with your real-life friends, family, neighbors, and church family.

Games promise relationships without the mess, a place to hide from the gaze of other people, a world where people can't hurt you. But they are no replacement for face-to-face fellowship. It might be messy, it might hurt at times, but we were made for real relationships. In fact, God has made us for eternal relationships. He has designed Christians to grow together with a family that we will be with for all eternity. I'm talking about the Church.

## A PLACE TO BE KNOWN

The primary places God designed us to have face-to-face fellowship is with our families, churches, and neighbors. Online friendships are fine, but when they begin to displace these primary relationships, something has gone wrong. We simply cannot live out our calling to our families, churches, or the unbelieving world if we cloister ourselves away within the safety of social simulations and the riskless relationships they offer.

In God's strength, we have to resist the urge to withdraw from real-life fellowship. How will you live a God-honoring life if you are hiding from the very people God created you to serve and be served by? How will you benefit from the grace of fellowship with other believers? How will you love your neighbor, much less reach them with the gospel, if your social world exists only in the cocoon of an online world?[2]

---

2    It is true that we can engage in evangelism through online games, and even fellowship with other believing gamers. Those are wonderful ministries. But we must be on guard against using those opportunities as an excuse to justify our neglect of

The sci-fi book *Ready Player One* by Ernest Cline describes a future where the world has gotten so bad, that everyone spends their days in a virtual reality world. They wear VR headsets and full-body suits called 'rigs' that allow them to be fully immersed in the simulated world. Eventually, the hero starts to realize that something is wrong with this escapist arrangement.

> *I'd come to see my rig for what it was: an elaborate contraption for deceiving my senses, to allow me to live in a world that didn't exist. Each component of my rig was a bar in the cell where I had willingly imprisoned myself.[3]*

That book is fiction, but the experience he described has very nearly become the reality for many people today. It was Cameron's reality. He sought freedom from the uncertainty and shame of in-person fellowship, but instead of escaping it, he hid from other people. I never saw Cameron again, but I pray to God that he eventually broke free of the prison he

---

the primary relationships God has given us in real life.

3  Ernest Cline, *Ready Player One*, (New York: Broadway Paperbacks, 2011), 215.

was constructing around himself and poured himself fully into the relationships God had given him.

## Main Point

*God created us for face-to-face fellowship with other people, so we should not settle for substitutes.*

## Questions for Reflection

- What are some of the most important relationships in your life?
- Why does God want us to have relationships with other people? What's the purpose?
- Why is it tempting to pull away from relationships with other people? Why do we sometimes feel like hiding?

# 5. Redeemed For Reward

===

*And without faith it is impossible to please him, for whoever would draw near to God must believe that he exists and that he rewards those who seek him.*
*(Heb. 11:6)*

Not only do games appeal to our desire for dominion and fellowship, but they are also attractive because they fulfill our longing for reward. This, like ruling and relationship, is part of God's design for mankind. But because of our sinfulness we often search for reward in the wrong places. We look for reward when we seek the approval of others, over-emphasize material success, or make idols of achievements.

Part of what makes a game a game is that it can be won. Every video game presents some opportunity for victory or reward. There's nothing like the feeling of posting a high score, defeating a difficult boss, or unlocking an achievement. It's the little highs of winning that keep us coming back for more. Like dominion and fellowship, that sense of attainment when we win is God-given. It's part of what motivates us in all our work. The Lord gave us a desire to work hard, overcome, and see the reward of our labors. The desire to do things for reward is a good thing. In fact, pursuit of reward is part of what drives our obedience to Christ.

## IT IS RIGHT TO SEEK REWARD

Saving faith is a trust in God's promise of salvation. It is the belief that God has done what He said He would do in sending Jesus Christ. When we believe in Jesus, we believe His promise that He will raise us to new life and give us an eternal inheritance. The Bible does not say our desire for heavenly reward is a bad motivation, it commends it: 'And without faith it is impossible to please him, for whoever would draw near to God must believe that he exists and that he rewards those who seek him.' (Heb. 11:6).

The whole story of Abraham, the man of faith, is about a guy who followed God because he believed God when He said He would reward him (Gen. 12:1–3; Heb. 11:11). God even uses that promise to reassure Abraham, saying his 'reward will be very great' (Gen. 15:1).

Our salvation is by grace through faith, and we cannot add anything to it by our good works (Eph. 2:8-9). Nevertheless, the Bible continually reiterates that righteousness will be rewarded in eternity (Ps. 19:11; 58:11; Prov. 11:18; Matt. 6:1-5; Col. 3:4). So, when Abraham followed God because of the promised reward that wasn't a sinful reason to obey, instead it is the very faith which is counted to him as righteousness (Gen. 15:6; Rom. 4:3; Gal. 3:6).

We will talk more about the reward for faithful stewardship in the next chapter, but for now you just need to understand that being motivated by, and finding pleasure in, reward is not a bad thing. It's how God has wired us.

Every human lives to seek a reward. The issue is what reward we are chasing after, and more importantly, from whom we are seeking it. When we look to God for the reward He has promised, we honor Him as trustworthy and faithful. But when we pursue lesser rewards as our chief aim—things like the praise of others, making a bunch of money, or video game achievements—something has gone terribly wrong in our thinking.

## WHY VIDEO GAME REWARDS KEEP US PLAYING

The promise of financial reward is what leads some people to become addicted to gambling, or workaholism. The promise of acclaim or praise from others causes some to worship at the idol of public approval. And the high of winning can likewise lead us to spending an unhealthy amount of time playing video games as we pursue the sense of achievement they give us.

The real allure of video games is that they enable us to enjoy those deep desires we were made to have – dominion, fellowship, and reward – but they do so by offering a version of reality which is not subject to the limitations of a fallen world. I can exercise dominion in a game without fear of failure. I can have relationships that can't hurt me because I'm able to hold them at arm's distance. And I am able to pursue reward without the sacrifice or risk that real-life rewards typically require. In this way video games offer us a substitute for the temporal and eternal rewards which God designed us to seek.

## VIRTUAL REWARDS ARE VIRTUALLY WORTHLESS

Temporal rewards are good. We were made to enjoy the reward of a hard day's work. Ecclesiastes 5:12 says, 'Sweet is the sleep of a laborer.' And just as God looked on the labor of His own hands after creating the world and He called it 'very good' (Gen. 1:31), so we who were made in His image enjoy a similar satisfaction when we stand back to look at a completed project, smile, and say, 'that looks good.'

This is what makes games so fun, overcoming obstacles, beating other players, or seeing our stats rise. But since it is all happening within a simulation, the things we accomplish in games don't really matter. When we win, we experience the feeling of reward, but there is no actual fruit to show for it. If we spend all our time chasing virtual rewards, therefore, we will be left empty-handed.

We must be careful that we don't trade the authentic battles of life, with their real rewards for the fake wars of video games and their paltry prizes.[1] It is this allure of reward without

---

1    Moore, Russell D. 'Fake Love, Fake War: Why so Many Men Are Addicted to Video Games and

risk that leads to the vices of passivity and addiction, and the never-ceasing search for the easy way in life. I'm afraid that just as with dominion, too many Christian students are enjoying the artificial rewards of video games to a degree that it is numbing their desire to seek those things which are above (Col. 3:1). Such a settling for easy rewards, if left unchecked, could result in a life of little ambition, where we always do the bare minimum and never live up to the potential God has created us for.

This is a tragic path for anyone, but especially so for Christians who have been put on an important mission by God (Matt. 10:16-18). We are to risk it all, to be ready to lay down our very lives for the cause of Jesus Christ, knowing that in the end our reward will be very great. The task is dangerous, but the reward will be worth it. We will look more at the subject of eternal reward in the next chapter.

## Main Point

*God designed us to work for eternal reward, but we can become distracted by the virtual rewards of video games.*

---

Internet Porn.' *The Journal of Discipleship & Family Ministry* 3, no. 1 (2012): 94–95.

## Questions for Reflection

- Have you ever felt empty after achieving something you'd worked really hard for in a game? Why do you think that was?
- Does it seem wrong to be motivated to do the right thing because of the reward? Why or why not?
- What is the reward believers in Jesus Christ look forward to?

# 6. It's Not Your Time to Waste

*You are not your own, for you were bought with a price. So glorify God in your body.*
*(1 Cor. 6:19b-20)*

By all accounts Brett's life was going great. He had completed his undergraduate degree, married his high school sweetheart, and landed his dream job. Brett was walking with the Lord, involved in his church, and even helped lead a Bible study. Brett was also an avid gamer.

In college he had been able to balance his studies and a part-time job with late-night gaming binges. And even though life had changed quite a bit since then, he was still able to make time for his favorite games. After dinner each night, Brett would kiss his wife goodnight and head to the den to play his favorite online game for an hour or two before coming to bed. His wife was fine with this arrangement and it worked out quite well for a while.

But as Brett became more involved in the game, he would be invited on dungeon parties, or need to spend a little more time finishing up a quest. Sometimes those evening sessions turned into late-night sessions, sometimes all-night sessions. As this developed into a pattern, he found himself increasingly tired at work the next day. Nothing an extra cup of coffee couldn't fix. But as this habit continued, he found himself less and less alert at work. And he even fell asleep at his desk a few times. Part of him knew this wasn't right, but he kept up the late-night gaming anyway, and the cycle continued.

As the quality of his work slipped, and his boss caught him asleep at his desk one too many times, Brett was eventually fired from his job. When his boss called him into his office to let him go, he told him exactly what Brett already knew: The company wasn't paying him to sleep at work, they were paying him to work. It wasn't his time to waste.

In this chapter, we will talk about the subject of stewardship, and specifically how we steward our time. Video games are not necessarily a waste of time, to say that would mean we'd have to say every hobby or form of entertainment is a waste of time. But any hobby, be it sports, politics, TV, or social media, can become a time waster. The best way to make sure you're not wasting time is to first understand whose time it actually is. The Bible teaches that we are stewards of God's resources, and when we waste our money, gifts, energy, or even time, we are really misspending things that belong to Him. Christians care about wasting time, because we recognize it's not our time to waste.

## THE PARABLE OF THE TALENTS

Jesus explained the principle of stewardship using the Parable of the Talents. Speaking about the Kingdom of Heaven, Jesus told the following story:

> *For it will be like a man going on a journey, who called his servants and entrusted to them his property. To one he gave five talents, to another two, to another one, to each according to his ability. Then he went away (Matt. 25:14-15)*

In the story, the man going on a journey represents God, the master of the house. The three servants represent followers of Jesus. Sometimes the servants are called 'stewards': that's where we get the concept of stewardship.

A steward is someone who is charged with looking after something that belongs to someone else. In this story, the master charges his servants to look after various amounts of money while he is away. Each is assigned an amount 'according to his ability' (15). The first two servants invest what was entrusted to them and make a handy return. 'He who had received the five talents went at once and traded with them, and he made five talents more. So also he who had the two talents made two talents more' (16-17).

But the third servant who had been entrusted with just one talent hoarded it like a grandma on a TLC special. 'But he who had received the one talent went and dug in the ground and hid his master's money' (18). The servant who buried the talent had no business doing that. It wasn't his money. He was supposed to invest what his master had entrusted to him and make a good return for him. That was his job. Instead of using the master's money to make more, however, he wasted it by letting it sit in the ground.

This is the heart of Christian stewardship: Whatever God has entrusted to you doesn't belong to you, but you are responsible to make good use of it for the Master. Whatever you have belongs to God, and He's loaned it to you so that you might bring glory to Him through it. 'You are not your own, for you were bought with a price. So glorify God in your body.' (1 Cor. 6:19b-20). This is why it's not just a bad idea, but actually wrong, to waste money, talent, or time. It's not just that we are failing ourselves, it's a failure to worship God as we ought to.

Just as you shouldn't waste your money on frivolous purchases or waste your talents on unworthy pursuits, you also shouldn't bury your time in video games. Because it's not your money, it's not your energy, and it's not your time to waste. God has entrusted these things to you so that you might glorify Him with them until He returns.

But like Brett, sometimes we slip into thinking that it really is our time. We think we can spend it however we want. But we're actually mismanaging something that belongs to God. When we over-indulge in video games, we aren't using God's time responsibly. But before you start thinking of stewardship as a burden, we need to look at the end of the Parable of the Talents where we see that it's actually in our own best interests to use God's resources God's way.

## THE REWARD FOR GOOD STEWARDSHIP

We might be tempted to think of stewardship as a burden, just another 'no' from God. But God is not a stingy master; as we saw in the last chapter He rewards those who serve Him with the resources with which they've been entrusted. In the long run, no one will ever complain that they got the short end of the deal for serving the Lord with their time. From the vantage point of eternity, when God rewards the righteous, every last one of us will wish we'd used our time even more wisely. Just look at how the parable ends:

*Now after a long time the master of those servants came and settled accounts with them. And he who had received the five talents came forward, bringing five talents more, saying, 'Master, you delivered to me five talents; here, I have made five talents more.' His master said to him, 'Well done, good and faithful servant. You have been faithful over a little; I will set you over much. Enter into the joy of your master.'(Matt. 25:19-21)*

When the Master returns to settle accounts, none of us will feel that any bit of the resources we invested for eternity was not worth it. In this parable, those who were faithful with a little were given much more. Jesus makes this principle explicit: faithfulness in this life will be rewarded in the next. Using God's resources wisely in this life is always a good investment.

So, yes, enjoy your video games, but enjoy them like a steward. Remember that it is good for us to rest and relax, but God has loaned us a limited amount of time and He intends for us to make good use of it. If you feel that you are spending too much of God's time on video games, maybe it's time to consider playing a little less and looking for what better ways you could invest that time for God's glory.[1]

## Main Point

*How we spend our time matters to God.*

---

1    For a deeper dive into the stewardship of time, check out one of Christian Focus' other titles: John Perritt, *Your Days Are Numbered: A Closer Look at How We Spend Our Time & the Eternity Before Us* (2016).

## Questions for Reflection

- How does seeing your time as a stewardship change the way you think about what you spend it on?
- What are some things other than video games on which you are tempted to waste time?
- What do you think the difference is between wasting time and getting the rest and relaxation you need?

# 7. Don't Glory in the Gore

*The Lord tests the righteous, but his soul hates the wicked and the one who loves violence.*
*(Ps. 11:5)*

When I talk to Christians about video games, normally they assume I'm going to go straight to the topic of violence. It is an important topic, but I consider the addictive potential of video games to be a matter of greater concern than the content in them, which is why I have dealt with that first.

I also know that students have a tendency to roll their eyes when I bring up the topic of violence in games. I used to as well. Hopefully, by now you can see that my objective is not to pour cold water on your fun. Instead, my aim is simply to cause you to evaluate everything in life, including your entertainment choices, by asking 'how can I most please God?'

We can be tempted to ignore concerns about violence in video games because of how overblown some of those criticisms have been in the past. But overreactions in the past do not warrant apathy in the present. If we want to walk as faithful followers of Christ, we should be willing to think deeply about whether the content of certain games is honoring to Him, and what effects our choice to be entertained by those kinds of things is having on souls.

## DO VIDEO GAMES MAKE YOU VIOLENT?

To understand why some parents, pastors, and teachers have such strong feelings about violence in games, it may be helpful to look at some history. Even back in the 70s and 80s, parents were raising concerns about the violence in pixelated arcade games.[1] The ESRB rating that you see on video games in the United States was actually a result of the hysteria over

---

1   The history of the arcade game *Death Race* from 1976 is one example of concerns over early video game violence. In the game players ran over 'gremlins' to score points. But to many observers the creatures you were being rewarded for running over looked disturbingly like humans.

violence in the 1992 game *Mortal Kombat* that culminated in a congressional hearing.[2]

But it was the 1999 Columbine school shooting that solidified the connection in people's minds between playing violent games and committing real-life violence. It was revealed shortly after that horrific shooting that the gunmen were fans of violent video games. In fact, just about any time a young person commits an act of mass violence, the media finds a way to bring up the role of violent video games.[3]

Since the Columbine shooting, there have been many studies done to try and formally prove a connection between playing violent games and doing violent actions. Most of those studies, however, have been unable to show a causal relationship between people who play violent video games and those who commit acts of violence in real life.

So, if violent video games don't make you violent, we don't need to worry about violence in the games we play, right? Well, actually, as

---

2    Kevin Schut, *Of Games and God: A Christian Exploration of Video Games* (Brazos Press, 2013), 53.

3    Ibid., 55.

Christians we still should care. Let me show you why.

It doesn't seem like video games actually cause violence. But that doesn't mean that they are good. As Christians, the question we should be asking is 'does my playing violent video games please God?' Our desire should not just be to avoid the things that most displease God, it should also be to want to do those things which most please God. This is a matter of the heart.

## AN ISSUE OF THE HEART

In Matthew 5:28 Jesus expands upon the command against committing adultery. The people in Jesus' day understood that one plain application of the commandment not to 'covet your neighbor's wife' was that it was wrong to have sex with someone you are not married to (Exod. 20:17). But Jesus pointed out that obedience to this command was about more than just the physical act. He said, 'But I say to you that everyone who looks at a woman with lustful intent has already committed adultery with her in his heart.' (Matt. 5:28). His point was that even people who fantasize about sleeping with someone who is not their spouse are still sinning. It's an issue of the heart. There are ways in which we can sin even though we aren't doing something physical. Lust is one of those ways, but it is not the only one.

For example, we know that the Lord commanded us not to murder (Exod. 20:8). But we shouldn't make the mistake that the people Jesus was talking to made, to think that as long as video games don't cause us to murder anyone then we are free and clear. That same principle from Matthew 5 applies here also. Jesus said even if we hate our brother, we are murderers at heart, whether or not we actually kill anyone (Matt. 5:22). Now, you may say, 'But I'm not hating anyone by playing these violent games.' But if you are acting out murder in your head, or make-believe murdering someone on a screen, what is your heart doing? There are of course different types of violence in games, it's not all murder. But if you are playing a game in which you are murdering people, do you really think God is pleased with that?

Have you ever considered why murder is bad in the first place? That may seem like a silly question, but the Bible actually tells us why murder is wrong. Murder is wrong because God made man in His own image (Gen. 9:6). When someone snuffs the life out of another image-bearer of God, it is not just a sin against the person being killed, it's a sin against the God in whose image he was made. If our aim is to please God, then even fictional acts of violence against fictional image-bearers of God, though they don't actually hurt anyone, may still be wrong. In our hearts we are pretending to do something that God finds abominable, and what's worse, we're doing it for entertainment.

## WHAT ABOUT VIOLENCE IN OTHER MEDIA?

I can already hear your objections to what I just said. 'Why does it always have to be about video games?' 'What about TV and movie violence, Reagan?' 'What about the Bible? It's full of descriptions of violent acts!' 'What about soldiers who have to kill people in real war? Can I not play war games? That's not murder.' Those are all great questions! And certainly, I do think it would be wise for Christians to more critically consider the content of all the entertainment we expose ourselves to. But maybe I can offer you a principle that will help you make these kinds of judgments for yourself in regard to all entertainment. Here's the principle: *Don't glory in the gore.*

There is a difference between the soldier who must, out of duty, kill to defend his country, and the soldier who actually finds enjoyment in the bloodshed. There's a difference between when the Bible describes violent acts, and when a horror movie revels in them. And there's a difference between when we play games in which we defeat bad guys, and when we play ones in which we gleefully roam around beating NPCs[4] to death with a baseball bat.

When we understand that bloodshed is not something fun to be entertained by, but that the only reason death exists is because of the sin of man, we should have a less casual attitude toward it. Psalm 11:5 says that God's 'soul hates the wicked and the one who loves violence.' Notice, it's not just the person who does violence, but the one who *loves* it. I never want to be a person who loves violence, even if it's make-believe violence.

It's also helpful to consider that there is a difference between watching a violent scene in a movie or reading about it in a book and you yourself being in control of it on a screen. In violent video games we aren't just passive observers of the violence, often we are the ones

---

4    Non-Player Character.

acting it out. This participatory nature of video games when it comes to violence should give us pause. The difference between witnessing fictional violence and choosing to commit it is a difference in the heart.

So, don't glory in the gore. Even if it is just fantasy bloodshed, be careful that you do not have feet that are swift to shed blood (Prov. 1:16). Instead, love the image of God in man, and hate what is evil. Keep your heart from taking joy in acting out, even in your imagination, things which God detests.

## SHOULD WE PLAY VIOLENT VIDEO GAMES?

So, should Christians play violent video games? I'm going to give a non-answer here and say, that depends. With so many types of video game violence, much of the answer depends on how we define violence. It is difficult, therefore, to give a blanket answer. But, as we have seen, the biggest consideration should be your heart.

We have to be honest with ourselves. Often, when we ask questions like this, we are looking for a way to defend a decision we've already made. If you're looking for an excuse to play a violent game, you'll come up with one.

But I would caution you to take seriously the nagging of your *conscience*. If a game doesn't seem right to you, there's no harm in being cautious and saying, 'You know what, I'm not going to play this game anymore.' I think the Lord would be very pleased by that kind of attitude. And isn't that what we want, to please the Lord?

## Main Point

*Christians should not enjoy the kinds of violence which God hates even if it's pretend.*

## Questions for Reflection

- Why does God hate murder?
- Why do you think people are sometimes drawn to violent movies or video games?
- Are there any games you play that you think might be causing you to glory in the gore? What are you going to do about that?

# 8. How Should We Think About Video Games?

---

*The wisdom of the prudent is to discern his way,*
*but the folly of fools is deceiving.*
*(Prov. 14:8)*

In light of what we've seen so far, what is the proper response of a Christian to video games? What should our overall attitude be toward gaming? In this chapter, we will look at three unhelpful responses Christians might have and a fourth approach that I believe is the most honoring to God.

## UNBIBLICAL LEGALISM

The first response to video games is so common that it's often caricatured in popular culture: the over-protective Christian mother who sees it as her sole mission to moralize society and protect her precious little ones from the wicked culture at all costs. To her, entertainment is the enemy, and it is her job to ensconce her babies in a bubble of protective ignorance.

That maternal impulse is certainly natural. God has designed mothers to protect their children. Likewise, we may encounter this protective attitude toward video games from fathers, pastors, and others who care about our spiritual well-being. And it is true that the world of entertainment is full of sinful content that can lure us away from a life of godliness.

Unfortunately, an overcautious attitude about video games can sometimes make people create a set of rules that go beyond the Bible, taking a broad brush to paint all video games as sinful. This then leads to a culture of judgementalism where anyone who does not abide by the same set of rules is labeled a sinner or looked down upon. This approach can also rob young people of the experience of exercising discernment.

Having certain household rules for video games is not wrong. Rules can function as guardrails against sinful content, but when a made-up rule is elevated to the same place as God's law, you've crossed the line into legalism. If we want to honor God in our approach to video games, we must be wary of slipping into unbiblical legalism. But we also must be careful not to overcorrect against this attitude and fall off the other side of the horse.

## UNCRITICAL PRAISE

In response to the prevalent attitude of unbiblical legalism about video games, some people have sprinted in the opposite direction. Out of a desire to defend against accusations that video games are inherently sinful, there has been a growing number of books and articles which instead want us to only see the good in video games. To these people, video games should be thought of in the same way that we might embrace a fine book, master painting, or an award-winning movie.[1] They are the works of culture, and only an uncivilized brute would find fault with them.

Others offer uncritical praise of games by extoling the many positive benefits of video games. They see themselves as apologists against even the most subtle warning about the dangers of gaming. They will emphasize how video games help develop problem-solving skills or keep kids from getting into drugs and

---

1   Ted Turnau, 'Let the Gamers Say 'Amen!,' *Christianity Today*, https://www.christianitytoday.com/ct/2013/april-web-only/let-gamers-say-amen.html.

other destructive behaviors. Essentially, they will point to any benefit of video games and use it to ignore all possible downsides. It is true that there are benefits to playing video games, but they need to be honestly weighed against the risks.

Like the first attitude of unbiblical legalism, uncritical praise is a refusal to exercise discernment when it comes to gaming. And as we've seen in previous chapters, like so many things in this God-created yet sin-sick world, gaming has both good and bad qualities. Therefore, Christians must approach them with wisdom.

## UNTHINKING APATHY

If I had to guess though, I would say most of us do not fall into either of those first two camps. We don't accept the unbiblical legalism, nor are we so naive as to think video games are worthy of uncritical praise. There are clearly both good and bad aspects to gaming. But the debate can be so confusing that sometimes the easiest position to take is one of unthinking apathy. The average believer has probably never given more than a passing thought to how video games affect them. They don't think video games are particularly bad or good.

They don't care, and frankly, they don't care that they don't care. This too is a problem.

The issue with this attitude is that it fails to take the Bible's warning about spiritual warfare seriously. 'Be sober-minded; be watchful. Your adversary the devil prowls around like a roaring lion, seeking someone to devour.' (1 Pet. 5:8). A wise believer is always on the lookout for Satan's deceptions. He knows that like bait on a mousetrap, our enemy tempts us with things that at first appear harmless and desirable. It's only once the trap has sprung that we realize our mistake.

We are in a spiritual war against a crafty enemy. If he can, the Devil will use things as seemingly benign as games to ensnare us with addiction, cause us to waste the time we've been charged to steward, draw our minds to sinful thoughts, and otherwise rob us of the joy of serving God and walking in holiness. This life is a spiritual war. We cannot close our eyes to it and apathetically skip through the minefield. What then is the proper response to video games? What should a Christian's attitude be?

## UNAPOLOGETIC DISCERNMENT

If unbiblical legalism, uncritical praise, and unthinking apathy are wrong ways to think about video games, what's the right way for a Christian to think about them? Well, we should think about video games the same way believers ought to think about everything in life, by turning to Scripture, exercising discernment, and asking God to show us what would most honor Him.

We need to approach video games with unapologetic discernment. I say unapologetic because sometimes we are overly concerned about what others think of us. *The enemy of discernment is the fear of man.* But we shouldn't worry about being lumped in with the kooky critics, the overzealous defenders, or those who are entirely indifferent about gaming. How you approach video games is a matter of wisdom between you and God. Our chief concern must be the heart, not what others will think of us. In considering how you will approach video games you may land on a conclusion that differs from those around you. That's okay. What matters is that you are open and honest before God with it and truly seeking to find the path that most honors Him.

A point of caution here: If you are under your parent's roof, you must remember that they may have a different opinion than you on video games. In such a case, you should defer to their decision, even if you disagree with it. To do so is to follow God's command to honor your father and mother (Exod. 20:12). Remember, your aim must never be to search the Scriptures for arguments to simply defend what you want to do, instead your goal must be to search God's Word to discover how best to serve and obey Him. If you utilize the arguments from this book not to foster healthy discussion, but to defy your parents or those God has put in authority over you, you will have missed the whole point. Honor God and those He has put in authority in your life, even if it means sacrificing something you enjoy.

As Christians our chief aim should be to bring God the glory He deserves. We want to walk in a way that is pleasing to Him and that requires us to align our hearts with His mission, to cast off every encumbrance. These are complex issues, but we have a sufficient Word and a God who has promised to give wisdom to those who ask for it (James 1:5). Discernment, when it comes to video games, is possible. God wants you to walk in holiness. He wants you to grow and to serve Him. And if you come with a humble heart genuinely seeking to know how to engage with video games in the way that most honors Him, He will make that clear.

In the next chapter, I will give you some principles and practical strategies for how to apply discernment to how you engage with video games.

## Main Point

*We should approach video games with an attitude of unapologetic discernment.*

## Questions for Reflection

- What are some of the good things you can learn from video games? What are some of the bad things?
- Did this chapter change the way you think about video games? Why or why not?
- Why is it important that we don't force our standards for video games onto other believers?

# 9. A Gameplan for Gaming

---

*So, whether you eat or drink, or whatever you do, do all to the glory of God.*
*(1 Cor. 10:31)*

We have covered a lot of ground in the last eight chapters. We've seen how video games are designed to keep us playing which can lead to addiction. Addiction can then keep us from fulfilling our God-designed mission and wasting the time we've been called to steward. We've observed how gaming can tempt our hearts by offering imitation rule, relationships, and reward. And we've also seen how the content of video games can lead to sin when we delight in things God hates.

With all of that in mind, in this final chapter, we will try and make a plan for how practically to approach gaming. Remember, this is a matter of wisdom. Each person may choose to approach video games differently. Your decision should be based on an honest evaluation of your own weaknesses and a desire to bring God the most glory with your life.

In order to arrive at a Christ-honoring approach to gaming, we'll look at three questions. When, what, and how:

1. When will you play video games and for how long?
2. What are the principles that will guide which types of games you will play?
3. How will you play these games when you do play?

If you can answer each of these questions clearly, you will have a game plan for gaming. But before we look at those three questions, there's one big question we have to answer first.

Will you play video games at all? You may already have come to the conclusion that given your own proclivities, you will quit video games altogether. That's a perfectly reasonable conclusion. If that is the case for you, own that decision, but don't look down on others who don't share that opinion.

But even if you haven't decided to abstain from video games, I would still encourage you to begin with laying video games on the altar. What I mean is seriously consider the option of quitting gaming all together. Before God, settle in your heart that you would be willing to give them up if you become convinced that is what would be most honoring to Him. As you evaluate the following questions, try and hold gaming with an open hand, and not with a defensive, white-knuckled grip. Your attitude should be one of humble submission to God; not my will but yours be done.

## WHEN GAMES?

If you decide you will play games, the next step is to decide in advance when you will play them. If in reading this book you felt convicted about how much time you spend on games, then it would be wise to make some adjustments in this area. Deciding in advance how much time you will play games is an exercise in self-discipline. You have to make some rules for yourself and stick with them. Making rules for yourself is not the same as legalism, as long as you understand that your rules are not God's laws. These are simply self-imposed guardrails to ensure the time doesn't get away from you.

I can't tell you how much time is too much. That's something you'll have to decide yourself. But consider getting counsel from others who know you well. Maybe you'll limit yourself to a certain amount of time each day. Or perhaps you will decide that instead of playing games every day, you'll only play for an hour in the evenings on certain days of the week. But whatever you decide, make a plan, write it down, and tell someone about it who can keep you accountable.

## WHAT GAMES?

Once you have decided when you will play games, the next question is what games will you play? Here we are dealing with the content of video games. If you think you might struggle with what we talked about in the chapter on glorying in the gore, then it might be wise to decide you won't play violent video games, or any game that tempts you to sin in your heart.

Read reviews of games you are considering playing to discover what content is in them prior to purchasing. Even still this sort of negative approach is difficult, since a lot of the information about content will not be discovered until you actually play the game. Sometimes you start playing a game that was recommended to you by another Christian only to be shocked by what's in it.

Instead of approaching games with the question of 'what games can't I play?' try asking the question 'what games should I play?' It's a positive rather than a negative approach. It assumes that unless you are confident that the content will not be detrimental to your walk with the Lord, then you won't play it at all.

This is the thinking of the apostle Paul who said in 1 Corinthians 10:23, 'all things are lawful, but not all things are helpful.' He was countering the excuses the Corinthians made for using their Christian freedom to do things that were not edifying for themselves or the church. Simply because something isn't bad, doesn't mean that it is good. Our Christian freedom is not an opportunity to indulge, but to serve without guilt or shame. We should evaluate our gaming choices with this same spirit. In everything in life, not just video games, we should certainly be asking 'will this hinder me?' but we should also be asking 'will this help me in my walk with the Lord?'

## HOW GAMES?
Lastly, you may decide that you are particularly drawn to the self-isolating effects of video

games, the fake fellowship we talked about in chapter four. In this case you may want to decide to only play games with other people. That is the decision I made when I realized my video game usage had gotten out of control, and I know several others who have made a similar commitment.

I don't play games by myself at all anymore. I don't keep games on my phone, computer, or other devices and I don't own a console. It's too tempting for me to get drawn back in, waste hours, avoid responsibilities, and hide from people. But I've found that if a friend wants to get together in person and play video games, it's an enjoyable way to have fellowship doing something I enjoy without the risk of being sucked back into unhealthy gaming habits.

The major thing you want to consider whenever you approach games, however, is where your heart is. Are you gaming to the glory of God? That should be the question that guides you in all of your thinking. Are you enjoying the common grace He's given us in games, or are you exposing yourself to content that tempts you to sin, shirking commitments, or being a poor steward of your life?

## YOU ARE NOT ALONE

Maybe through reading this book you've come to realize that you have an unhealthy relationship to video games. Maybe you are enslaved by them, or you know the content of your favorite games is not pleasing to God, or maybe you recognize that you are wasting God's time by the number of hours you are putting into video games. The weight of conviction over that can be heavy. And sometimes even though we want to quit something, we find it difficult to make changes. This can be discouraging. But you need to know that you are not alone.

We read in 1 Corinthians 10:13 that 'no temptation has overtaken you that is not common to man. God is faithful, and he will not let you be tempted beyond your ability, but with the temptation he will also provide the way of escape, that you may be able to endure it.' The point of that verse is that temptation is not something unique to you. Sure, video games are newer technology, but the temptations they present are the same as Christians have always faced. Your exact circumstances may differ, but your struggle is not unique to you. And that's good news.

If you feel hopefulness in your fight, notice what that verse says, 'God is faithful... he will also provide a way of escape.' There is a way out. There is freedom from addiction, isolation, and time wasting. That freedom is what God wants for you. And since your struggle is not unique, I urge you not to try and fight this battle alone. Seek help from a parent, pastor, or Christian friend. And above all bring it to the Lord in prayer and ask for His supernatural wisdom and power.

## CONCLUSION

God has given us this world to enjoy for His glory. And He has given men and women wisdom to make wonderful creations and technologies that can bring us great enjoyment. Video games are not evil, but like so many good things, they can ensnare us and cause us to lose focus on what really matters most. You were created to glorify God; don't let video games knock you off that mission.

So whether you eat or drink (or game) or whatever you do, do it all to the glory of God.

## Main Point

*We may not all approach video games the same way, but we should decide in advance how much we will play and what types of games.*

## Questions for Reflection

- Have you decided to stop playing games all together? Why or why not?
- When will you play video games? How frequently? For how long?
- What standards will you use for determining which video games you will play?

# Appendix A: What Now?

- Give thanks that God has not only given you the necessities of life, but also things to enjoy and be entertained by like video games. Because every good gift comes from God (James 1:17).
- Get a piece of paper and track how many hours you spend gaming each week. Include games on your phone, console, and computer.
- Challenge yourself to take a week off from gaming.
- Go through all of the games you have. Ask God for wisdom to recognize if any of the games have content that would be dishonoring to Him.
- Think about the types of games you most enjoy. Then, brainstorm some hobbies you might try in the real world that have some of the same features. For example, if

you like building games consider taking a woodworking class or reading a book on architecture.

- Get involved in a small group or Bible study at your church. Invest yourself in deep Christian friendships and fellowship.
- If you think you might be addicted to video games, ask your parents, a pastor, or a mentor at your church for help.
- Make prayer and Bible reading a daily part of your life. Ask God for the desire to do it. Find a Bible reading plan and pick a time and place you will do it every day.
- Get out into creation with your friends. Go for a hike, play a sport, or plan a camping trip. Real life has better graphics than any game.
- Come up with some personal rules to keep your gaming in check. For example, 'only one hour of gaming per day' or 'I'll only game on the weekends.'

# Appendix B: Other Books on this Topic

Challies, Tim, *The Next Story: Life and Faith after the Digital Explosion* (Zondervan, 2011)

Crouch, Andy, *The Tech-Wise Family: Everyday Steps for Putting Technology in Its Proper Place* (Baker Books, 2017)

Perritt, John, *Your Days Are Numbered: A Closer Look at How We Spend Our Time & the Eternity Before Us* (Christian Focus, 2016)

Reinke, Tony, *12 Ways Your Phone is Changing You* (Crossway, 2017)

Welch, Edward, *Addictions: A Banquet in the Grave: Finding Hope in the Power of the Gospel* (P&R, 2001)

Reformed Youth Ministries (RYM) exists to reach students for Christ and equip them to serve. Passing the faith on to the next generation has been RYM's passion since it began. In 1972 three youth workers who shared a passion for biblical teaching to youth surveyed the landscape of youth ministry conferences. What they found was an emphasis on fun and games, not God's Word. Therefore, they started a conference that focused on the preaching and teaching of God's Word. Over the years RYM has grown beyond conferences into three areas of ministry: conferences, training, and resources.

- **Conferences:** RYM's youth conferences take place in the summer at a variety of locations across the United States and are continuing to expand. We also host parenting conferences throughout the year at local churches.

- **Training:** RYM launched an annual Youth Leader Training (YLT) conference in 2008. YLT has grown steadily through the years and is offered in multiple locations. RYM also offers a Church Internship Program in partnering local churches as well as youth leader coaching and youth ministry consulting.
- **Resources:** RYM offers a variety of resources for leaders, parents, and students. Several Bible studies are offered as free downloads with more titles regularly being added to their catalogue. RYM hosts multiple podcasts: *Parenting Today*, *The Local Youth Worker*, and *The RYM Student Podcast*, all of which can be downloaded on multiple formats. There are many additional ministry tools available for download on the website.

---

If you are passionate for passing the faith on to the next generation, please visit www.rym.org to learn more about Reformed Youth Ministries. If you are interested in partnering with us in ministry, please visit www.rym.org/donate.

# Christian Focus Publications

Our mission statement —

STAYING FAITHFUL

In dependence upon God we seek to impact the world through literature faithful to His infallible Word, the Bible. Our aim is to ensure that the Lord Jesus Christ is presented as the only hope to obtain forgiveness of sin, live a useful life and look forward to heaven with Him.

Our books are published in four imprints:

### CHRISTIAN
## FOCUS

Popular works including biographies, commentaries, basic doctrine and Christian living.

### CHRISTIAN
## HERITAGE

Books representing some of the best material from the rich heritage of the church.

## MENTOR

Books written at a level suitable for Bible College and seminary students, pastors, and other serious readers. The imprint includes commentaries, doctrinal studies, examination of current issues and church history.

## CF4•K

Children's books for quality Bible teaching and for all age groups: Sunday school curriculum, puzzle and activity books; personal and family devotional titles, biographies and inspirational stories — because you are never too young to know Jesus!

Christian Focus Publications Ltd,
Geanies House, Fearn, Ross-shire,
IV20 1TW, Scotland, United Kingdom.
www.christianfocus.com
blog.christianfocus.com